On a Tropical Island

Written by Sarah Irvine

The Caribbean

My name is Paz. I live on the tropical island of Jamaica in the Caribbean. Many different plants and animals live in Jamaica. How do you think they came to the island?

Contents

Look for the **Activity Zone!**
When you see this picture, you will find
an activity to try.

Journey to Jamaica

Welcome to Jamaica! This tropical paradise is the third largest island in the Caribbean, yet it is only about 146 miles long and 50 miles wide. Although it is one of many Caribbean islands, it has its own geography and wildlife. Hundreds of rivers and waterfalls run down the mountains, and many caves wind their way through the soft, limestone ground. Lush rainforests are home to many different plants and animals, some of which are found nowhere else on Earth. The hot weather, white sandy beaches, and coral reefs attract thousands of tourists every year.

Jamaica has warm weather all year round. Many tourists from countries farther north visit Jamaica during the winter to get a break from the cold.

geography   the layout of the physical features of an area

The Caribbean

The Caribbean is divided into three main island groups:

1. The Bahamas—about 3,000 small islands and reefs

2. The Greater Antilles—the large islands of Cuba, Jamaica, Puerto Rico, and Hispaniola (Haiti and the Dominican Republic)

3. The Lesser Antilles—smaller islands divided into two groups: the Leeward Islands and the Windward Islands

Jamaica's many waterfalls and rivers carry rainwater from the inland mountains to the sea.

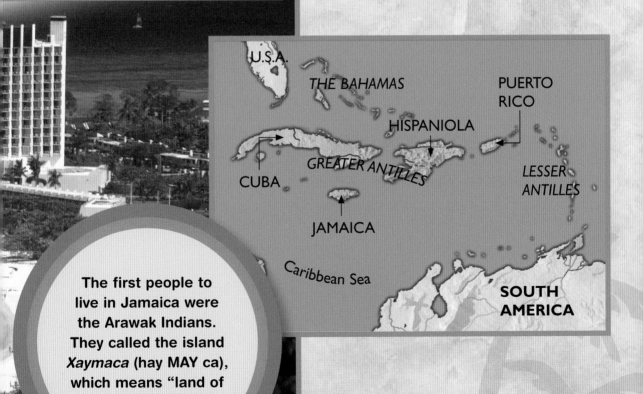

U.S.A.

THE BAHAMAS

PUERTO RICO

HISPANIOLA

GREATER ANTILLES

CUBA

LESSER ANTILLES

JAMAICA

Caribbean Sea

SOUTH AMERICA

The first people to live in Jamaica were the Arawak Indians. They called the island *Xaymaca* (hay MAY ca), which means "land of water and wood."

Underwater Mountains

Many scientists believe that Jamaica and the other islands in the Greater Antilles are volcanic islands. They are the tips of large, underwater volcanoes that formed millions of years ago. They probably formed when two of Earth's plates (large pieces of Earth's hard, outer crust) collided, creating volcanic eruptions.

Mountains cover more than half of Jamaica and are important to the country's economy. They are a source of bauxite, an ore of aluminum, and are also good places for growing crops, such as coffee.

ore   a mineral that is partly made up
      of something useful, such as a metal

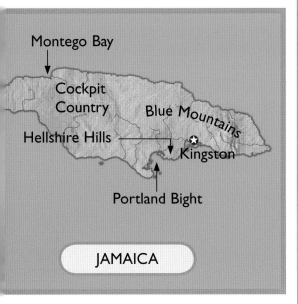

Montego Bay

Cockpit Country

Hellshire Hills

Blue Mountains

☆ Kingston

Portland Bight

JAMAICA

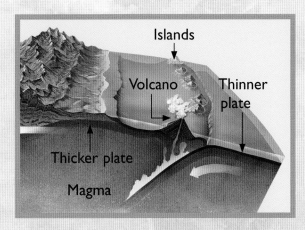

Islands

Volcano

Thinner plate

Thicker plate

Magma

When two of Earth's plates meet and one goes under the other, this is called *subduction*. The thinner plate is pushed under the thicker one, and the rock melts into magma. The magma then rises to the surface in volcanic eruptions. This process can create an arc-shaped chain of volcanic islands along the edge of the plate. The Greater Antilles are an island arc.

Coffee is a major industry in Jamaica. Coffee plants grow well on the slopes of the Blue Mountains. There, the temperature is cooler than at sea level, and mists keep the plants and soil damp all year round.

The highest point in Jamaica is Blue Mountain Peak. It is 7,401 feet high. Many hikers climb a trail to the top in the dark so they can watch the sun rise.

Cockpit Country

Many of the mountains in the Caribbean are covered in thick layers of limestone. The limestone formed at times when the sea level was higher. Over millions of years, the skeletons of tiny sea creatures accumulated on top of the volcanic rock and slowly hardened into limestone.

Limestone is softer than many other rocks and can be worn away, or eroded, by rainwater. Rugged terrain formed by the erosion of limestone is known as *karst*. The Cockpit Country in Jamaica is one of the best examples of a karst area in the world. Water erosion has created large cave systems, rolling hills, underground rivers, and sinkholes.

In caves, the minerals in dripping water slowly accumulate into long, thin cones. Those that hang down are called *stalactites*; those that project up from the cave floor are called *stalagmites*.

accumulate   to build up

A sinkhole is created when the roof of an underground cavern collapses. Sinkholes occur in many places. They can even appear in towns and cities.

This tourist guide is pointing out limestone stalactites hanging from the roof of a cave in Cockpit Country.

Limestone Caves

Limestone caves take thousands of years to form. Rainwater, which contains a gas called *carbon dioxide*, mixes with underground water, forming an acid that very slowly dissolves the rock.

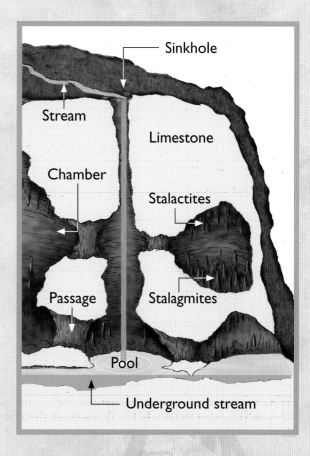

A Tropical Climate

Jamaica is a tropical island. It is close to the equator, which means it lies on the part of Earth that is closest to the Sun all year around. The temperature is usually about 80°F in the summer and drops to only about 75°F in the winter. Like all islands, Jamaica's climate is affected by the ocean, which produces humid air, clouds, and rain.

Jamaica has wet seasons and dry seasons. During the wet seasons, large, rotating storms called *hurricanes* form in the warm, tropical oceans and move through the Caribbean. They create extreme weather conditions that can cause a great deal of destruction on the islands.

The drier months in Jamaica are usually July and August and from December to April.

humid   air with a lot of water vapor

How Hurricanes Form

In September 2004, Jamaica was struck by Hurricane Ivan. Strong winds of up to 165 miles per hour and huge waves battered the island. Thousands of people were left without shelter, food, electricity, or running water.

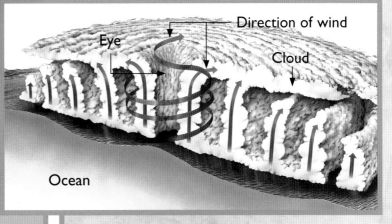

Direction of wind

Eye

Cloud

Ocean

A hurricane begins as a cluster of thunderstorms over warm water. The warm water heats the air above it, which rises, creating tall banks of clouds. The clouds begin to spin, or rotate, as they are blown by the wind. They move over the warm ocean, gaining more and more energy.

As the warm air rises, cool air, high in the sky, is sucked down the middle of the clouds to take the place of the warm air. This channel of cold air is called the *eye of the storm*. As it passes overhead, there is a short period of calm weather with no rain.

From Rock to Forest

When an island first forms, there are no plants or animals living on it. Wildlife must move to the new island from other land areas, such as nearby continents or other islands.

Seeds are often transported to an island by wind, birds, or ocean tides. The first creatures to live on an island are usually birds that fly and animals that swim, such as seals. Slowly, more plants grow, and more animals come to the island. In time, they develop populations that interact in a unique way, creating what scientists call an *ecosystem*.

Coconuts are palm-tree seeds. They can float to new islands. Often, small insects will hitch a ride on a seed.

unique   the only one of its kind

Ecological Succession

Scientists believe there is a natural process that builds a new ecosystem. It is called *ecological succession.*

- The first plants that grow on bare ground are soon followed by animals that come to feed on the plants.

- As the plants grow, they create shade and protection from wind, and when they die, they help build up the soil layer. This allows other kinds of plants and animals to move in.

- These newer plants and animals compete with the existing plants and animals for space and food. In time, a balance is achieved—the ecosystem is established.

Large land animals usually cannot reach new islands on their own. Animals such as pigs and horses did not reach Jamaica until Europeans brought them in the 1500s. Other animals, such as rats that found their way onboard ships, were brought by accident.

Island Ecosystems

The plants and animals in an ecosystem are linked by their feeding relationships. Plants use energy from the Sun to produce their own food. When an animal eats a plant, the energy stored in the plant is passed on to the animal, providing it with the energy to live and grow. Some of this energy is then passed on to any animal that eats that animal. This is called a *food chain*. Each ecosystem has many different food chains. These chains link up to form complex food webs.

In the Jamaican rainforests, thousands of species of plants, birds, reptiles, and amphibians interact with introduced animals to create a unique food web.

Primary consumer—an herbivore, or plant-eating animal

Producer—plant

Jamaica is home to some of the smallest birds in the world—hummingbirds. The doctor bird, or streamertail hummingbird, is Jamaica's national icon.

Secondary consumer—a carnivore, or meat-eating animal

This food web shows the feeding relationships of some of the plants and animals in Jamaica. Study its structures; then create a simple food web for some of the plants and animals that live near you.

Jamaican iguanas   Plants

Rats

    Mongooses

Pigs

Hutias   Wild dogs

Cattle

    Cats

Horses

Bats   Jamaican boas

Skinks

Frogs   Insects

Birds

    Plankton

Fish

Crayfish   Crocodiles

15

Native to Jamaica

Island ecosystems are very delicate, because they are small, isolated, and unique. Often, the wildlife communities became established long before people introduced new plants and animals from other places. New species of plants can take over land where native plants once grew, reducing the amount of food available for animals. New species of animals can prey on native species or steal their food. Many rare species have no means of protecting themselves from these new predators. Species are especially likely to become extinct on an island, because the populations are small, and they have nowhere else to move to.

Most mammals cannot fly or swim, so there are few native mammals in Jamaica. However, several species of native bats live in the island's caves.

The rare hutia is the only land mammal endemic to Jamaica. This guinea-piglike rodent lives in a burrow and eats plants.

endemic native to a particular place and found only there

What Is Biodiversity?

Jamaican tody, a species endemic to Jamaica

The more species of plants and animals that live in a country, the greater is its biodiversity. Jamaica has a high level of biodiversity; many different plants and animals live there. There are more than 3,000 different plant species. There are also many different species of birds, bats, and insects. However, very few large land animals are native to the island.

The Jamaican Iguana

During the 1800s, settlers introduced many predators, such as cats, rats, dogs, and mongooses, to the island of Jamaica. A native reptile, the Jamaican iguana, was thought to have become extinct because of attacks from new predators and loss of its habitat. However, in 1990, a very small population of Jamaican iguanas was discovered in the remote and rugged Hellshire Hills. A recovery project was started to save the few remaining iguanas and help them to breed. Fifteen years later, biologists estimate the population of iguanas to be between 150 and 200.

Each year, about 20 baby Jamaican iguanas are caught and raised in zoos. They are released back into the wild when they are big enough to defend themselves —at about 5 to 12 years old. Since the program began in 1996, 76 iguanas have been released.

Biologist Rick Van Veen's job is to learn about and protect Jamaican iguanas. He uses tracking devices to find individual iguanas.

South Camp (above) is where Rick is based for most of the year. He lives in a hut and sometimes sleeps under the stars in an insect dome. The camp is remote, so Rick needs to bring in plenty of food and water. Local wildlife visit the camp, including an iguana that steals vegetables from Rick's garden!

Every three days, Rick checks, clears, and baits about 60 traps set to catch predators of the iguana, such as this mongoose. The traps have a door that shuts when an animal steps on a pressure plate.

The iguana grows to about five feet long and is Jamaica's largest endemic land animal. It is one of the rarest animals in the world.

Eye on the Environment

Introduced species aren't the only problem that can threaten delicate island ecosystems. People can cause other problems when they build towns, farms, factories, and mines. Industrial waste can pollute rivers and coastal waters. Many of Jamaica's native trees have been cut down to sell overseas and to make room for farms and towns. As a result, many native animals have lost their homes, and the exposed, bare soil has been washed away by rainwater. Sometimes exotic trees have been planted to replace the forests. However, some of these trees cannot withstand hurricanes, and they can be dangerous when they fall over during extremely high winds.

Waste products from bauxite mining created this sludge pond in Jamaica.

exotic   plants or animals brought to a country from another place

Islands within Islands

The people of Jamaica are working hard to protect their island. The Portland Bight Protected Area is a region of 724 square miles of forests, wetlands, and coral reefs. Here, efforts are being made to create a place where wildlife and people can live together.

More than 75 percent of the forests in Jamaica have been cleared. Jamaica is not wealthy, and timber brings money to the economy. However, the country is losing its forests at a fast rate; it is said to have one of the highest rates of deforestation in the world. The remaining areas of forest are small and scattered around the island. This has created small islands of habitat that separate native plants and animals from others of their species. Sometimes the forest areas become too small for certain animal and plant populations to survive.

habitat the place where an animal or plant lives

Tourist Hotspot

Each year, millions of tourists visit the Caribbean. The money from tourism is good for the economy; it helps provide jobs for people and money to build houses, schools, hospitals, and roads. However, tourists increase the population, use resources that are limited, and increase the amount of garbage on the island. Today, places for tourists to stay and visit are carefully planned so they don't damage the beaches and landscape. Cruise ships are carefully monitored so they don't pollute the ocean with their fuel.

More than 2,500,000 people live in Jamaica. Every year, nearly a million tourists add to the number of people on the island.

Coral Reefs

There are many coral reefs in the Caribbean. Reefs are important structures. They provide homes for many sea creatures, and they change carbon dioxide in the air into oxygen, which animals need to live. Coral reefs are damaged by such things as water pollution, overfishing, and people walking on them. In Jamaica, some people are now trying to help save the reefs.

Find Out More!

1. What animals are native to the place where you live? What animals have been introduced from other places?

2. On many other islands around the world, native species now have to compete with introduced species. Pick an island and find out about the wildlife living on it.

To find out more about the ideas in *On a Tropical Island*, visit **www.researchit.org** on the web.

Index